## Purchasing Tips

- A 1½- or 2-quart slow cooker is the perfect size for one or two people.

- Choose one with different heat settings (high, low, warm).

- Oval cookers will hold two larger pieces of food side by side without overlapping (such as chicken breast halves).

- Round cookers are especially good for soups, casseroles, and baked items.

- A removable crock or insert makes clean-up easier.

## Cooking Tips

- Thaw meat and vegetables before placing in slow cooker.

- Unless directed otherwise in a recipe, keep the slow cooker's lid on during cooking to avoid heat loss.

- When food is done cooking, reduce heat to "warm" setting to hold until serving time. Prevent excessive moisture build-up by lining lid with paper towels.

- Food cooks best when the slow cooker is filled ½ to ⅔ full. If the insert isn't full enough, food will cook faster.

- Cooking times are approximate; monitor your own cooker's heat and adjust accordingly.

- Some recipes can be cooked equally well on high or low power. It takes about twice as long to cook on low as it does on high.

- To avoid cracking a cooker's insert, do not expose it to sudden temperature changes.

- To prevent curdling and ensure a creamy texture, limit the length of time you slow cook fresh dairy products or add them near the end of cooking time.

- Refrigerate any leftovers promptly.

fills 2 bowls

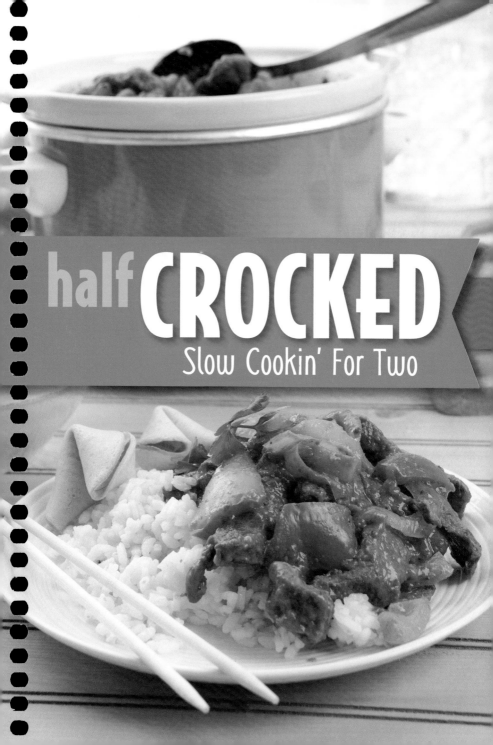

# half CROCKED

## Slow Cookin' For Two

Printed in the United States of America
by G&R Publishing Co.

Distributed By:

507 Industrial Street
Waverly, IA 50677

ISBN-13: 978-1-56383-479-0
ISBN-10: 1-56383-479-0
Item #7085

# Apricot Oatmeal

## Ingredients

¾ C. steel-cut oats

½ C. chopped dried apricots*

2 T. currants

1 C. evaporated or soy milk

1 tsp. vanilla extract

Ground cinnamon

\* Or try dried pears, apples, cherries, or a combination of dried fruits.

## Directions

In a 1½-quart slow cooker, combine 1 cup water, oats, apricots, currants, evaporated milk, and vanilla; stir well.

Cover and cook on low for 8 to 9 hours or until tender and thick. Sprinkle lightly with cinnamon and serve hot with desired toppings.

## Add-ons...

Top with vanilla yogurt, half & half, honey, brown sugar, maple syrup, nuts, apricot preserves, or fresh fruit for added flavor.

fills 6 tortillas

# Cheesy Salsa Chicken

## Ingredients

- 2 boneless, skinless chicken breast halves
- 1½ tsp. taco seasoning
- ½ C. salsa
- ½ (10.7 oz.) can nacho cheese soup (about ½ C.)
- ¼ C. sour cream, plus more for serving
- 6 flour tortillas or tortilla chips
- Lettuce, onions, tomatoes, shredded Cheddar cheese

## Directions

Place chicken in a 1½-quart oval slow cooker. Sprinkle evenly with taco seasoning. In a small bowl, stir together salsa and soup; pour over chicken.

Cover and cook on low for 6 to 8 hours.

Remove chicken from cooker and shred meat. Return shredded meat to cooker and stir in sour cream. Serve on tortillas with lettuce, onion, tomatoes, shredded Cheddar, and sour cream, or keep warm and serve as a hearty dip with tortilla chips.

## Serve it whole...

*After cooking, set each chicken breast half on a bed of rice (do not shred). Stir sour cream into sauce mixture and drizzle it on top. Sprinkle with shredded Cheddar.*

# Vegetarian Minestrone

1½ C. vegetable broth

⅔ C. diced tomatoes

⅓ C. kidney beans, drained and rinsed

¼ C. each diced onion and celery

½ C. sliced baby carrots

½ C. frozen green beans, thawed

½ tsp. minced garlic

1 tsp. minced fresh parsley

¼ tsp. each salt and dried oregano

⅛ tsp. each black pepper and dried thyme

½ C. cooked elbow macaroni

1 C. chopped baby spinach

1 to 2 T. shredded Romano cheese

fills 2-3 bowls

low 6-8 hrs.

2 qt.

# Directions

In a 2-quart slow cooker, combine vegetable broth, tomatoes, kidney beans, onion, celery, carrots, green beans, garlic, parsley, salt, oregano, black pepper, and thyme. Stir well.

Cover and cook on low for 6 to 8 hours.

Approximately 15 minutes before serving, stir in cooked macaroni and spinach; cover and cook on low until heated through (spinach wilts). Divide among serving bowls and sprinkle with Romano.

## Add meat...

*Place a sliced onion and a 1- to 1½-lb. beef roast in a small slow cooker; season with salt and black pepper. Cover and cook on low for 8 to 10 hours. Shred the meat and add to this soup, or slice and serve as desired.*

**Slow-Cooked Roast Beef**

serves 2

1½ qt.

# Barbecued Ribs

## Ingredients

1½ to 1¾ lbs. pork baby back ribs

Salt and black pepper to taste

½ C. ketchup

¼ C. chili sauce

½ C. finely diced onion

2 T. brown sugar

1 T. distilled white vinegar

½ tsp. dried oregano

½ tsp. Worcestershire sauce

Dash of hot pepper sauce

## Directions

Cut ribs into two equal slabs (about 3 ribs each) and arrange in a 1½-quart oval slow cooker. Season with salt and black pepper. Cover and begin cooking on high.

Meanwhile, in a small bowl, mix ketchup, chili sauce, onion, brown sugar, vinegar, oregano, Worcestershire sauce, and hot sauce. Pour sauce mixture over ribs and turn to coat well.

Cover and reduce heat to low; cook for 7 to 9 hours or until tender. Skim off accumulated grease. Serve ribs with sauce.

## Sauce it...

*Prepare sauce as directed, but pour it over other meats in a slow cooker, such as chicken, ham, pork chops, or beef roast. Cook on low until tender and fully cooked.*

fills 2 bowls

# Ham & Bean Soup

## Ingredients

- ⅔ C. dried great northern beans (soaked overnight)
- 2 C. chicken broth
- ⅓ C. diced ham
- ½ C. chopped onion
- ¼ C. grated carrot
- ¼ C. chopped celery
- 2 T. chopped celery leaves
- ¼ tsp. chili powder
- 1 bay leaf
- Garlic salt and black pepper to taste

## Directions

Drain and rinse soaked beans. In a 1½ quart slow cooker, combine beans, chicken broth, ham, onion, carrot, celery, celery leaves, chili powder, and bay leaf.

Cover and cook on low for 6 to 8 hours. Discard bay leaf and season with garlic salt and black pepper before serving.

## To soak beans...

*Sort through dry beans, removing any damaged ones or small stones. Rinse beans in a colander. Transfer to a bowl, cover with fresh water, and let soak overnight (at least 8 hours). Remove any floating beans; drain and rinse before cooking.*

serves 2

14

**1½ qt.** low 3½-5 hrs.

# Bacon-Apple Chicken

## Ingredients

- 2 boneless, skinless chicken breast halves
- 4 bacon strips
- ½ C. barbecue sauce
- 2 T. brown sugar
- 1 T. lemon juice
- 1 large Gala apple, peeled and chopped

## Directions

Wrap each chicken breast half with two bacon strips and place side by side in a 1½-quart oval slow cooker.

In a small bowl, mix barbecue sauce, brown sugar, lemon juice, and apple. Pour sauce mixture over chicken.

Cover and cook on low for 3½ to 5 hours or until chicken is cooked through.

## Shred it...

*Shred the cooked chicken and fill pita pockets or buns. Drizzle with some of the apple-barbecue sauce and serve with shredded cabbage or lettuce and condiments as desired.*

fills 5 small buns

# Meatball Sliders

## Ingredients

- 8 oz. frozen meatballs (about 15 small), thawed
- ½ C. tomato sauce
- ½ C. diced tomatoes with green chilies
- ¼ tsp. garlic powder
- 2 tsp. chopped fresh parsley
- 5 slider buns
- Sliced provolone cheese

## Directions

Place meatballs in a 2-quart slow cooker. Pour tomato sauce and tomatoes with juice over meatballs. Sprinkle evenly with garlic powder and parsley.

Cover and cook on high for 3 hours. Serve on buns with provolone and a little sauce.

**Meatballs & Pasta**

## Or do this...

*Serve meatballs and sauce over your favorite cooked pasta and sprinkle with freshly grated Romano or Parmesan cheese.*

# Italian Potatoes

½ small onion, thinly sliced

2 large russet potatoes, peeled

½ small green bell pepper, sliced

Salt and black pepper to taste

1 tsp. Italian seasoning

⅔ C. spaghetti sauce

1 C. shredded Italian cheese blend, plus more for sprinkling

Grated Parmesan cheese

serves 2-3

# Directions

Place half the onion in a 2-quart slow cooker.
Slice potatoes into thin rounds. Layer half the potato
slices over onions, followed by half the bell pepper
slices. Season with salt and black pepper; sprinkle
with ½ teaspoon Italian seasoning. Spread with
half the spaghetti sauce and half the Italian cheese.
Repeat layers.

Cover and cook on low for 3½ to 5 hours or until
potatoes are tender.

Near end of cooking time, sprinkle additional
Italian cheese and Parmesan on top; cover and cook
10 minutes more.

## *Main dish...*

*Add layers of sliced pepperoni (approximately 1½ oz.)
and/or ½ lb. browned, drained Italian sausage; slow
cook as directed.*

serves 2

**1½ qt.**

# Shrimp Creole

## Ingredients

¾ C. diced celery

½ C. chopped onion

⅓ C. diced bell pepper

½ C. tomato sauce

1 (14.5 oz.) can diced
   tomatoes

½ tsp. minced garlic

½ tsp. Creole seasoning,
   or to taste

¼ tsp. salt

⅛ tsp. black pepper

2 to 3 drops hot pepper
   sauce

½ lb. frozen cooked
   shrimp, thawed

Cooked brown or white
   rice or angel hair pasta

## Directions

In a 1½-quart slow cooker, combine celery, onion, bell pepper, tomato sauce, tomatoes with juice, garlic, Creole seasoning, salt, black pepper, and hot sauce; stir well.

Cover and cook on high for 3 to 4 hours.

During the last 15 to 30 minutes of cooking time, stir in shrimp and reduce heat to low. Cover and cook until shrimp is just heated through. Serve over hot rice or pasta.

## Want it thicker?

*Before adding shrimp, sauce may be thickened with a mixture of 1½ tsp. cornstarch dissolved in 1 T. cold water. Stir into sauce, cover, and cook on high until thickened.*

fills 2-3 bowls

# Turkey-Wild Rice Soup

## Ingredients

- ½ C. chopped onion
- ½ C. diced celery
- ½ C. sliced baby carrots
- ½ C. diced smoked turkey
- ¼ C. uncooked wild rice, rinsed
- ½ tsp. dried tarragon
- ¼ tsp. black pepper
- 1¾ C. chicken broth
- ½ C. frozen peas, thawed
- ¾ C. evaporated milk
- 2 T. flour

## Directions

Coat a 1½-quart slow cooker with cooking spray. Place onion, celery, carrots, turkey, and wild rice in cooker. Sprinkle with tarragon and black pepper. Pour chicken broth over all.

Cover and cook on low for 4 to 6 hours or until vegetables and rice are tender. Stir in peas; cover and cook on low for 15 minutes or until heated through.

In a small bowl, whisk together evaporated milk and flour until smooth; stir into soup. Cover and cook for 10 minutes more or until thickened.

## Wild rice...

*should be rinsed in cold water before cooking. This dark-colored grain takes longer to cook than white or brown rice. When fully cooked and tender, the kernels will swell and pop open.*

serves 2-3

low 6-7 hrs.

1½ qt.

# Beef Stroganoff

## Ingredients

¾ lb. beef stew meat, cut into 1″ pieces

⅓ C. chopped onion

1 (10.7 oz.) can golden mushroom soup

1 (4 oz.) can sliced mushrooms, drained

⅛ tsp. black pepper

¼ tsp. minced garlic

Dash of Worcestershire sauce

½ C. sour cream

Cooked noodles, rice, or mashed potatoes

## Directions

In a 1½-quart slow cooker, stir together beef, onion, soup, mushrooms, black pepper, garlic, and Worcestershire sauce.

Cover and cook on low for 6 to 7 hours or until meat is very tender. Just before serving, stir in sour cream until well blended and creamy. Serve over hot noodles, rice, or mashed potatoes.

## Hold it...

*Not quite ready to eat? Turn your slow cooker to "keep warm" setting to hold the stroganoff a bit longer. However, don't stir in the sour cream until just before serving.*

serves 2

# Glazed Sweet Potatoes

## Ingredients

½ C. orange juice

1 T. cornstarch

2 T. butter, melted

Dash of salt

⅓ C. brown sugar

1 (15 oz.) can sweet
  potatoes, drained

## Directions

In a 1½-quart slow cooker, mix orange juice and cornstarch until dissolved. Stir in butter, salt, and brown sugar. Add sweet potatoes and toss to coat.

Cover and cook on high for 3 hours. Turn off heat, stir gently, and let rest at least 10 minutes to allow glaze to thicken.

## Fresh and sweet...

*Peel and slice 2 or 3 medium sweet potatoes and place in a buttered 1½- to 2-quart slow cooker. Prepare glaze mixture as directed (or substitute apple cider for the orange juice); pour over potatoes and toss lightly. Cover and cook on low for 5 to 7 hours.*

# Stuffed Peppers

2 large bell peppers, any color

⅔ C. frozen soy crumbles,*
  thawed

¼ C. finely chopped onion

½ tsp. minced garlic

1 C. tomato sauce

¼ tsp. each salt and
  ground cumin

⅛ tsp. ground cinnamon

Dash each black and
  cayenne pepper

⅓ C. uncooked couscous

Shredded Cheddar or Monterey
  Jack cheese

serves 2

# Directions

Coat a 1½-quart oval slow cooker with cooking spray; set aside.

Cut off the stem end of each pepper and remove top, seeds, and membranes. Rinse and drain peppers. In a medium bowl, combine soy crumbles, onion, garlic, tomato sauce, salt, cumin, cinnamon, black pepper, and cayenne pepper; mix well. Stir in couscous. Spoon half of mixture into each pepper. Pour ½ cup water into prepared cooker and set peppers upright inside.

Cover and cook on low for 4 to 6 hours or until peppers are tender. Sprinkle with cheese before serving.

## *What's this?

*Soy crumbles offer a no-cook vegetarian alternative to ground beef. If you prefer, brown ½ lb. ground beef in a skillet, drain, and rinse before combining with other ingredients. Black beans and/or whole kernel corn may also be added.*

# Jerked Pulled Pork

½ tsp. chili powder

¼ tsp. ground allspice

⅛ tsp. each garlic powder, salt, and black pepper

Dash each ground nutmeg, thyme, and cayenne pepper, or to taste

2 T. lime juice

1 (1 to 1¼ lb.) pork tenderloin

1 small onion, sliced

1 C. barbecue sauce

2 T. dark rum

4 large hamburger buns

serves 2-4

# Directions

In a small bowl, combine chili powder, allspice, garlic powder, salt, black pepper, nutmeg, thyme, and cayenne pepper. Drizzle lime juice over tenderloin and then rub spice mixture into meat. Place meat in a zippered plastic bag; seal and refrigerate at least 3 hours or overnight to marinate.

To cook, place onion in a 1½-quart slow cooker. Remove tenderloin from marinade and cut into two or three even chunks. Set meat on onions in cooker. In a small bowl, whisk together barbecue sauce and rum; pour over meat.

Cover and cook on low for 8 to 10 hours or until meat is fork tender.

Remove pork from cooker and shred meat. Return shredded meat to cooker and stir until coated; cook until heated through, about 15 minutes. Serve meat and onions on buns with additional sauce on the side, if desired.

## Or slice it...

*For sliced pork, shorten cooking time to approximately 6 hours. Slice the meat, drizzle with sauce and onions, and serve with Hash Brown Casserole (recipe on page 32).*

**Jerked Pork Tenderloin**

serves 2

# Hash Brown Casserole

## Ingredients

- ⅓ C. sour cream
- ⅓ C. cream of mushroom soup with roasted garlic (from a 10.7 oz. can)
- ⅓ C. shredded American cheese, plus more for sprinkling
- 2 T. finely chopped onion
- ⅛ tsp. each salt and black pepper
- 2 C. frozen Southern-style hash browns, thawed

## Directions

Coat a 2-quart slow cooker with cooking spray; set aside.

In a medium bowl, stir together sour cream, soup, cheese, onion, salt, and black pepper. Add hash browns and toss to coat. Spoon mixture into prepared cooker.

Cover and cook on high for 1½ hours. Reduce heat to low and cook 1½ hours more.

## Flavor twists...

*Try other soup flavors such as cream of chicken or nacho cheese. Use frozen O'Brien potatoes and party dip in place of hash browns and sour cream. Top casserole with other cheeses like Cheddar, Monterey Jack, or Mexican blend.*

fills 2-3 bowls

# Black Bean-Tortilla Soup

## Ingredients

1 C. black beans, drained and rinsed

1 C. chicken stock or broth

½ C. salsa

½ C. frozen whole kernel corn, thawed

Dash of hot pepper sauce

½ tsp. minced garlic

½ tsp. dried oregano

⅛ tsp. ground cumin

¾ C. cooked, shredded chicken

1 tsp. lime juice

½ C. shredded Cheddar cheese

1 T. chopped green onion

Sour cream and tortilla strips

## Directions

In a 1½-quart slow cooker, stir together beans, chicken stock, salsa, corn, hot sauce, garlic, oregano, and cumin.

Cover and cook on high for 2½ to 3½ hours.

Before serving, stir in chicken and lime juice; cover and cook on high until heated through, about 20 minutes. Divide among serving bowls and sprinkle with cheese and green onion. Top with sour cream and a few tortilla strips.

## Quick chick...

*Use one 4.5 oz. can chunk chicken in place of cooked, shredded chicken.*

serves 2-3

1½ qt.

# Cheesy Potatoes & Ham

## Ingredients

1½ C. frozen O'Brien potatoes, thawed

1 C. diced cooked ham

1 C. shredded Cheddar cheese

1 C. frozen cut green beans, thawed

1 (10.7 oz.) can cream of potato soup

Dash of onion powder

¼ C. shredded carrot, optional

¼ C. sour cream

Chopped fresh chives

½ C. French-fried onions

## Directions

Coat a 1½-quart slow cooker with cooking spray. In cooker, stir together potatoes, ham, Cheddar, green beans, soup, onion powder, and carrot, if desired.

Cover and cook on low for 5 to 6 hours.

Toward end of cooking time, stir in sour cream and chives. Sprinkle onions over the top. Cover and cook 5 minutes more or until onions are just heated through.

## Shortcuts...

*Purchase the ham, cheese, and carrots already diced or shredded. Omit the onion powder and fresh chives by using chive and onion-flavored sour cream.*

# Asian Orange Chicken

¼ C. finely chopped onion

2 boneless, skinless chicken breast halves, cut into strips*

½ red and/or green bell pepper, cut into strips

3 T. orange juice

½ tsp. orange zest

1 tsp. brown sugar

1 to 2 tsp. finely sliced candied ginger

½ C. orange marmalade

1 tsp. soy sauce

2 T. barbecue sauce

Dash of garlic powder

Cooked rice or couscous

serves 2

# Directions

In a 2-quart slow cooker, layer half the onion, half the chicken, and half the bell pepper strips; repeat layers.

In a small bowl, mix orange juice, orange zest, and brown sugar; pour over chicken. Sprinkle ginger on top.

Cover and cook on high for 3 hours or until chicken is almost cooked through.

Drain juices from slow cooker and reduce heat to low. In a small bowl, stir together marmalade, soy sauce, barbecue sauce, and garlic powder; pour over chicken. Cover and cook 30 minutes more or until chicken is done. Serve over hot rice or couscous.

*\* Or buy ½ to ¾ lb. boneless, skinless chicken breast strips.*

## Slow Cooker Rice...

*In a buttered 1½-qt. slow cooker, mix 1 C. rice, ¼ tsp. salt, and scant 2 C. water. Cover and cook on high about 2 hours, stirring once. Reduce heat to warm, line lid with a paper towel to absorb moisture, and let rest 30 to 60 minutes. Fluff with a fork before serving.*

# Pizza Pasta Casserole

1½ C. uncooked spiral pasta

¼ lb. very lean ground beef

¼ C. each chopped onion and red bell pepper

½ tsp. minced garlic

⅓ C. sliced, quartered pepperoni

¼ C. sliced olives (black or green)

¾ C. shredded mozzarella or pizza cheese blend, divided

1 C. pizza sauce

Grated Parmesan cheese

serves 2-4

1½ qt.

# Directions

Coat a 1½-quart slow cooker with cooking spray. Rinse pasta in hot water and place in cooker. Crumble uncooked ground beef into cooker. Add onion, bell pepper, garlic, pepperoni, olives, and ¼ cup mozzarella; stir to combine and set aside.

In a small bowl, mix pizza sauce and ¼ cup water. Pour sauce over mixture in cooker and stir well.

Cover and cook on low for 3½ to 4 hours or until pasta is tender.

Toward end of cooking time, sprinkle with remaining ½ cup mozzarella; cover and let melt. Sprinkle with Parmesan just before serving.

## Rice is nice...

*In the slow cooker, combine 1 C. uncooked rice, 1½ C. pizza sauce, and 1¼ C. water. Stir in mushrooms, olives, onion, bell pepper, and pepperoni as desired. Cover and cook as directed above or until liquid is absorbed and rice is tender. Stir once and sprinkle with mozzarella; let melt before serving.*

**Pizza Rice**

# Beef Stew

1 lb. beef stew meat

2 medium potatoes, peeled

2 medium carrots, peeled

¼ C. flour

½ tsp. salt

¼ to ½ tsp. black pepper

1 tsp. onion powder

½ tsp. each garlic powder and paprika

1½ C. beef broth

½ tsp. Worcestershire sauce

¼ tsp. dried oregano

1 bay leaf

fills 2 bowls

# Directions

Cut stew meat and potatoes into 1˝ chunks and cut carrots into ¾˝ pieces; set aside.

In a large zippered plastic bag, mix flour, salt, black pepper, onion powder, garlic powder, and paprika. Add beef chunks and seal bag; shake until meat is evenly coated. Transfer to a 1½-quart slow cooker and top with potatoes and carrots.

In a small bowl, mix beef broth and Worcestershire sauce; pour over vegetables and meat. Sprinkle with oregano and top with bay leaf.

Cover and cook on low for 5 to 7 hours or until meat and vegetables are tender. Turn off heat; remove bay leaf and stir gently. Let rest for 10 minutes to thicken gravy before serving.

## Over 'taters...

*Omit potatoes when cooking the stew and serve the meat and carrot mixture over baked or mashed potatoes instead. Top with shredded Cheddar.*

**Stew-Topped Spuds**

fills 2-3 bowls

# Split Pea Soup

## Ingredients

- 1 C. dried split green peas
- ½ C. each diced onion, carrot and celery
- 3 C. chicken or vegetable stock, or more as needed
- 1 bay leaf
- ½ tsp. salt
- ¼ tsp. each black pepper, dried thyme, and dried parsley
- Pinch of dried rosemary
- ¼ lb. Polish sausage or diced ham

## Directions

Place peas in a 1½-quart slow cooker. Add onion, carrot, celery, chicken stock, and bay leaf. Stir in salt, black pepper, thyme, parsley, and rosemary. Be sure liquid covers peas (add more if needed).

Cover and cook on low for 8 to 10 hours or until peas reach desired tenderness. For a creamy soup, lightly puree mixture with an immersion or regular blender.

Toward end of cooking time, grill or heat the sausage and slice as desired. Add to soup in cooker; cover and cook about 20 minutes more. Remove bay leaf before serving.

## Go meatless...

*Make the soup with vegetable broth and omit the sausage. Stir in some smoked paprika for added flavor.*

# Loaded Tater Tot Bake

2 to 2½ C. frozen mini tater tots, thawed

¼ lb. Canadian bacon slices, halved

½ C. chopped onion

¾ C. shredded Cheddar cheese

2 T. grated Parmesan cheese

3 eggs

¼ C. half & half

1 T. flour

Salt and black pepper to taste

Real bacon bits

serves 2

low 4 hrs.

# Directions

Coat a 1½-quart slow cooker with cooking spray.
Place one-third of the tater tots in cooker, followed
by one-third each of the Canadian bacon, onion,
Cheddar and Parmesan. Repeat layers two more
times; set aside.

In a small bowl, whisk together eggs, half & half,
and flour until smooth. Season with salt and black
pepper. Pour evenly over layers in cooker and
sprinkle bacon bits over the top.

Cover and cook on low about 4 hours or until
cooked through.

## Add-ins...

*Change it up with different meats such as sliced pre-
cooked sausage links and other cheeses, or add chopped
bell peppers and sliced mushrooms.*

# Pepper Steak

¼ C. flour

½ tsp. garlic powder

¾ lb. beef sirloin steak, sliced into strips

½ medium onion, thinly sliced

1½ tsp. soy sauce

1½ tsp. sesame or vegetable oil

½ tsp. brown sugar

3 T. tomato sauce

½ tsp. beef bouillon granules dissolved in 1 T. hot water

Salt and black pepper to taste

½ each green and red bell pepper, sliced or chunked

Cooked rice or mashed potatoes

serves 2-3

# Directions

In a large zippered plastic bag, mix flour and garlic powder. Add beef strips and seal bag; shake until meat is evenly coated. Place onion and meat in a 1½-quart slow cooker; set aside.

In a small bowl, mix soy sauce, oil, brown sugar, tomato sauce, and bouillon water. Pour over meat in cooker and stir to combine.

Cover and cook on low for 5 to 7 hours. During the last 1 to 2 hours of cooking time, stir in bell peppers and continue to cook until meat is tender and peppers reach desired doneness. Serve over hot rice or mashed potatoes.

## Shortcut...

*Purchase pre-sliced stir-fry beef or ask your grocer to slice the steak into strips for you.*

# BBQ Pork Chops

2 (1″ thick) boneless loin
   pork chops*

½ small onion, sliced

¼ tsp. garlic powder

½ C. barbecue sauce

2 tsp. cornstarch, optional

*If chops have been "butterflied," fold in half
  before placing in cooker.*

serves 2

# Directions

Trim excess fat from pork chops. Place most of the onion slices in a 1½-quart oval slow cooker and set chops on top, side by side. Arrange remaining onion slices over chops and sprinkle with garlic powder; pour barbecue sauce over all.

Cover and cook on low for 4 to 5 hours or until meat is cooked through.

Remove chops to a serving platter and keep warm. If desired, thicken sauce by dissolving cornstarch in 1 tablespoon water; stir into sauce from cooker and microwave on high for 1 to 2 minutes until thickened, stirring once. Serve sauce with pork chops.

## Serve with...

*Garlic Smashed Potatoes. In a 2-qt. slow cooker, combine 3½ C. diced red potatoes, 3 tsp. minced garlic, and 1 C. chicken broth. Cover and cook on high for 3 to 4 hours. Drain potatoes, reserving liquid. Add 2 T. butter, 2 oz. cream cheese, and 3 to 5 T. half & half to potatoes and mash well, adding reserved liquid as needed. Season and keep warm until serving.*

**Garlic Smashed Potatoes**

# Mexican Egg "Bake"

¼ C. chopped onion

4 frozen precooked sausage patties, thawed

½ tsp. minced garlic

½ C. diced bell pepper, any color

¾ C. shredded Pepper Jack or Mexican cheese blend, plus more for serving

5 eggs, lightly beaten

2 to 3 T. chopped green chiles (from a 4 oz. can)

½ tsp. chili powder

Dash of cayenne pepper

Salt and black pepper to taste

Salsa, sour cream, fresh cilantro, and/or black olives, optional

serves 2-3

# Directions

Coat a 1½-quart slow cooker with cooking spray. Place onion in cooker. Crumble sausage over onion. Top evenly with garlic, bell pepper, and ¾ cup cheese; set aside.

In a medium bowl, whisk together eggs, chilies, chili powder, cayenne pepper, salt, and black pepper. Pour egg mixture over ingredients in cooker.

Cover and cook on low for 3 to 4 hours or until set and cooked through. Serve with salsa, sour cream, fresh cilantro, and black olives as desired.

## Olé!

*Build your own breakfast burritos when you scoop the cooked Mexican Egg Bake onto flour or whole wheat tortillas. Serve with red or green salsa, sour cream, and other toppings as desired.*

**Breakfast Burritos**

# S'mores Brownies

2½ T. butter

2 T. plus ½ C. mini milk
    chocolate chips, divided

1 egg

¼ C. sugar

½ tsp. vanilla extract

3 T. flour

1½ tsp. unsweetened
    cocoa powder

Dash of salt

3 or 4 graham cracker squares

¾ C. mini marshmallows

serves 4

# Directions

Line a 1½-quart slow cooker with foil and coat with cooking spray; set aside.

Melt butter and 2 tablespoons chocolate chips together; stir and let cool. In a medium bowl, beat together egg, sugar, and vanilla; whisk in melted chocolate. Stir in flour, cocoa powder, and salt until blended. Pour half the batter into prepared cooker. Cover batter with a layer of graham cracker squares, breaking and piecing together as needed. Sprinkle remaining ½ cup chocolate chips over crackers and top with remaining batter.

Cover and cook on low for 3 to 4 hours or until firm. Remove brownies from cooker by lifting foil; let cool on foil.

Before serving, sprinkle marshmallows over brownies. Set foil with brownies under broiler for 30 to 60 seconds or until marshmallows are toasted. Watch closely to avoid burning. Cool slightly before cutting.

## Check 'em...

*Brownies may look undercooked in the center even when done. If brownies buckle when foil is lifted, cook longer and check every 15 minutes until firm enough to remove.*

# Stuffed Apple Duo

¼ C. brown sugar

2 T. dried sweetened
   cranberries or raisins

2 T. chopped pecans

1 tsp. ground cinnamon

⅛ tsp. ground allspice

Dash of salt

2 large apples*

2 T. butter

½ C. cranberry-apple juice
   or water

Ice cream or whipped
   topping, optional

serves 2

# Directions

In a small bowl, stir together brown sugar, cranberries, pecans, cinnamon, allspice, and salt; set aside.

With a knife or melon baller, cut out each apple's stem and core, leaving bottom of apples intact to hold fillings. Enlarge holes near the top and peel off a narrow strip of apple skin around openings. Stuff each apple with half the brown sugar mixture, poking it down firmly to make room for more filling. Top each apple with 1 tablespoon butter. Pour juice into a 1½-quart oval slow cooker and set stuffed apples upright inside.

Cover and cook on low for 6 to 7 hours or until fork tender. To serve, drizzle apples with remaining sauce from cooker and serve warm with ice cream or whipped topping, if desired.

\* *Try Rome, Crispin, McIntosh, Jonagold, Golden Delicious, Pink Lady, or Granny Smith apples.*

## Caramel twist...

*Try stuffing each apple with 2 T. brown sugar, 3 cinnamon red-hot candies, 1 T. butter, and 1 or 2 unwrapped caramels. Sprinkle lightly with cinnamon and cook with apple juice until tender.*

serves 4

1½ qt.

# Caramel Rum Fondue

## Ingredients

1 (14 oz.) pkg. caramels, unwrapped

⅔ C. heavy cream

½ C. mini marshmallows

1 T. rum (or ½ tsp. rum extract)

Assorted dippers (apple wedges, strawberries, donut holes, cubes of cereal-marshmallow treats, gingersnaps, vanilla wafers, Nutter Butters, shortbread cookies)

Waffle bowls, optional

## Directions

Lightly coat a 1½-quart slow cooker with cooking spray. Place caramels and cream in cooker.

Cover and cook on low for 1½ to 2 hours or until melted, stirring occasionally.

Stir in marshmallows and rum. Cover and continue cooking on low (or warm setting) 20 to 30 minutes more. Keep warm and serve with assorted dippers in edible waffle bowls, if desired.

## Add a treat...

*For more fun, dip caramel-coated foods into scrumptious toppings like coconut, chopped peanuts, chopped raisins, toffee bits, mini chocolate chips, or chopped M&Ms.*

# Blueberry Cobbler

¼ C. plus 1 T. flour, divided

2 T. plus ¼ C. sugar, divided

¼ tsp. baking powder

Salt

Pinch each of ground cinnamon and ground nutmeg

1 egg

1½ tsp. milk

1½ tsp. vegetable oil

1 C. fresh or frozen blueberries, thawed

3 T. brown sugar

¼ C. quick oats

1½ T. butter

2 T. chopped pecans

serves 2-4

# Directions

Coat a 1½-quart slow cooker with cooking spray. In a small bowl, combine ¼ cup flour, 2 tablespoons sugar, baking powder, dash of salt, cinnamon, and nutmeg; set aside.

In another bowl, whisk together egg, milk, and oil; add to flour mixture and stir until moistened. Spread batter in prepared cooker. In a medium bowl, combine remaining 1 tablespoon flour, remaining ¼ cup sugar, and dash of salt. Add blueberries and stir until coated; scatter evenly over batter in cooker.

Cover and cook on high for 1½ to 2 hours or until cobbler tests done with a toothpick.

Meanwhile, mix brown sugar and oats. Cut in butter until crumbly; stir in pecans. Sprinkle mixture over cobbler; cover and cook on high 15 to 20 minutes more. Uncover and let rest 10 minutes before serving.

# Fresh ideas...

Use fresh seasonal berries, such as raspberries, blackberries, or a combination of your favorites. Serve with frozen yogurt, ice cream, or whipped cream.

# Orange Cheesecake

6 T. chocolate wafer cookie crumbs

4 T. sugar, divided

1½ T. butter, melted

5 oz. cream cheese, softened

1 egg

1 T. frozen orange juice concentrate

¼ tsp. orange flavoring

½ tsp. orange zest, plus more for garnishing

1½ tsp. flour

¼ tsp. vanilla extract

Fudge ice cream topping

serves 2

# Directions

Place one or two metal canning jar rings in the bottom of a 1½-quart slow cooker to act as a riser during cooking. Set a 4˝ springform pan on top to check fit; remove pan and set aside.

In a small bowl, mix crumbs, 1 tablespoon sugar, and butter. Pat into bottom and partway up sides of springform pan; set aside. In another bowl, beat together cream cheese and remaining 3 tablespoons sugar until creamy. Add egg and beat for 3 minutes. Add juice concentrate, orange flavoring, ½ teaspoon orange zest, flour, and vanilla; beat 2 more minutes. Pour mixture into crust and set pan on riser in cooker.

Cover and cook on high for 2 to 2½ hours or until firm around edges (center should still jiggle slightly when pan is lightly shaken).

Turn off heat and let rest for 1 hour or until pan is cool enough to remove. Run a knife around edges to loosen cheesecake. Cool completely before removing sides of pan. Chill. Before serving, drizzle with fudge topping and garnish with more orange zest.

## Or do this...

*Instead of a chocolate crust, make it with graham cracker or vanilla wafer crumbs. Before serving, top cheesecake with whipped cream, orange zest, and mandarin oranges.*

# *Index*